JACK AND BOBBY

JACK AND BOBBY

Tom Murphy

MetroBooks

MetroBooks

An Imprint of Friedman/Fairfax Publishers

©1998 by Michael Friedman Publishing Group, Inc.

Library of Congress Cataloging-in-Publication Data

Murphy, Tom
    Jack and Bobby / by Tom Murphy.
        p.   cm.
    ISBN 1-56799-591-8
    1. Kennedy, John F. (John Fitzgerald), 1917-1963—Pictorial works.
2. Presidents—United States—Biography—Pictorial works.
3. Kennedy, Robert F., 1925-1968—Pictorial works. 4. Legislators—
United States—Biography—Pictorial works. 5. United States.
Congress. House—Biography—Pictorial works. I. Title.
E842.1.M87   1998
973.922'092'2—dc21   98-7886

Editor: Ann Kirby
Art Director: Jeff Batzli
Designer: Eddy Herch
Photography Editor: Amy Talluto
Production Director: Karen Matsu Greenberg

Color separations by Bright Arts Graphics (S) Pte Ltd
Printed in Italy by Poligrafiche Bolis SPA

10 9 8 7 6 5 4 3 2 1

For bulk purchases and special sales, please contact:
Friedman/Fairfax Publishers
Attention: Sales Department
15 West 26th Street
New York, NY 10010
212/685-6610 FAX 212/685-1307

Visit our website:
http://www.metrobooks.com

I know him by his harp of gold,
Famous in Arthur's court of old.
I know him by his forest dress,
The peerless hunter, harper, knight...

—*Tristram & Iseult*, Matthew Arnold

Many thanks to all the people who supported me throughout this, my first project with MetroBooks. My name is on the cover, but their work is inside. And thanks to the Kennedys for being heroes at a time when heroes were desperately needed.

INTRODUCTION

Volumes have been written, and thousands of hours of film and video have been produced to satisfy the public's hunger to know more about the lives of Jack and Bobby Kennedy, two brothers whose commitment to public service set standards toward which those aspiring to enter the political arena still strive today. Their lives were the stuff of myth: they were handsome, wealthy, and good, and they were martyred, cut down in their prime by the forces of evil. So the legend goes, and what is most remarkable of all is that the legend—tempered by the fundamental fact that they were first, last, and always human beings—was largely true.

They came to the fore, youthful, vigorous, and visionary, guiding a country just emerging from the chill complacency of the Fifties and the isolationism of the Cold War, and brought the spark of idealism to a nation hungry for a dream. They challenged Americans to be bold, compassionate, and united, at a time when the country was bitterly divided by poverty and racism. They brought the arts to the forefront of American consciousness, and made the United States a world nation.

Jack was the political prodigy: the first Roman Catholic and the youngest president ever elected, though mature-looking beyond his years. He was the ultimate public figure: handsome, charming, and married to a glamorous American aristocrat. Bobby was the private Kennedy, the family man, working tirelessly behind the scenes to assure his brother's election, then again in the powerful but unglamorous position of attorney general of the United States. He was intense, hot-tempered, and—especially after the assassinations of his brother and of Dr. Martin Luther King, Jr.—driven to heal the nation and bring it into the light of equality and justice.

John Fitzgerald Kennedy, born in 1917, was the second child and second son of Joseph Patrick Kennedy, the grandson of poor Irish immigrants who over two generations had achieved the American dream. Born into the comfortable middle class, Joe amassed a fortune, constructed a brilliant network of power and influence, and rose to be ambassador to Britain, the nation's highest diplomatic post. Joe Kennedy intended his daughters to marry well, and his sons to be leaders. Jack was born to politics on both sides of the family: His mother, Rose, was the daughter of former Boston mayor John "Honey Fitz" Fitzgerald.

Robert Francis Kennedy, born in 1925, was the seventh of Joe Sr.'s nine children, and the third boy. With an eight-year difference between Jack and Bobby, the two boys were not close as children. Though public service was a family tradition, Joe pinned his greatest hopes on his firstborn and namesake, and indeed, Joe Jr. was a golden boy, excelling in everything he turned to, whether scholastic pursuits or athletics. Though his younger brothers, encouraged to do their best, succeeded in stretching their capabilities, it seemed they could never compete with their father's eldest son.

In 1944, after the Allied invasion of Normandy, Joe Jr. was killed on a bombing mission. The family was devastated, and in their grief Jack and Bobby became closer. Two years after Joe Jr.'s death, Jack won a seat in the House of Representatives (he would serve two subsequent terms), and his campaign style said much about his future political style. Rather than relying on the traditional Democratic Party structure, Jack depended upon his private circle of friends and relations. After he was elected to the House, he followed an equally independent, nonpartisan, rather conservative course (he once candidly declared himself "not a liberal"), both in foreign affairs and racial policies. Yet, once in office, he began to move toward a more idealistic agenda, especially in the area of civil rights for African Americans.

Jack was a war hero, whose modesty about the PT 109 episode ("They sank my boat.") endeared him to millions. Frankly ambitious, he literally aimed for the stars, creating a space program that continues today. Though a vocal proponent of nuclear disarmament, he was equally frankly anti-Communist, which led him into the debacle of the Bay of Pigs Invasion, and the larger pitfall of Vietnam, which later administrations would escalate into a national disaster. He established the Peace Corps, which would expose thousands of young Americans to the realities of the world outside their doors. And in time, the youth, glamor, and increasingly genuine idealism of his administration inspired the press to dub it Camelot, and when it ended with a gunshot, a stunned nation grieved and raged.

The brothers, a study in contrasts, completed each other. Jack was polished and charming, with a mature manner that made him at home with world leaders. Bobby, with his trademark shock of hair, always looked boyish, and his open admiration of his models—whether Jack himself or Dr. King, Jr.—added to his youthful air. Their behavior with respect to the hearings conducted by Senator Joseph McCarthy is emblematic of their styles. In a letter later made public, Jack expressed a concern about "the menace of communism within our borders," but balanced this with a commitment to the principle of a person being innocent until proven guilty. By contrast, when Bobby was assistant counsel to the Senate permanent subcommittee on investigations, chaired by McCarthy, he resigned after joining Decmocratic senators in a protest against McCarthy's methods. Where Jack gradually moved toward a more liberal position on desegregation, motivated by moral considerations, Bobby's increasingly passionate pursuit of racial equality arose from a profound empathy for African Americans and the poor as individuals, as well as an ardent desire for justice.

Bobby interrupted his own career to run Jack's 1952 campaign for the Senate. In 1960, after serving three years on the Senate Select Committee on Improper Activities in the Labor or Management Field, Bobby again left, this time, to manage Jack's presidential campaign. Displaying his deep respect for

and profound understanding of his younger brother, Jack appointed Bobby attorney general, the position that allowed Bobby to set a clear course for the nation and implement his vision of a just society. During the three years of Jack's presidency, the brothers became closer than ever before.

Shattered by Jack's murder, Bobby emerged from a period of deep mourning with his ideals revitalized, undergoing a second radicalization after the death of his other hero, Dr. Martin Luther King, Jr. In the wake of the assassinations, and given his disinclination for the limelight, Bobby's decision to run for president was clearly heroic, and equally manifestly the result of a simple—though surely not easy—yes-or-no decision. In the end, Jack's and Bobby's heroism was not the stuff of legends, but rather the expression of their integrity and of intimately felt beliefs, and in that way, like the daily heroism of ordinary people.

To those who remember, this book will bring back the excitement, promise, and heartbreak of Camelot. To those exploring this period in American history for the first time, this introduction will, we hope, convey a sense of this epic time of hope and tragedy, of challenge and achievement. A time that united the American people. A time unlike any other.

PART ONE
A FAMILY ALBUM

The Kennedy family's rags-to-riches story, only three generations after they arrived in Boston as refugees of Ireland's potato famine in 1848, is a living example of the American Dream. Ambitious and proud, the patriarch of the Kennedy clan, Joseph P. Kennedy, Sr., was determined to become a millionaire before the age of thirty-five and to have one of his sons rise to prominence in American politics. On both counts, he succeeded several times over.

Both Jack Kennedy and Bobby Kennedy were born into a charmed, privileged existence, but the ethic of work and service instilled in them by their father would not allow them to view the world merely as their playground. They were expected to excel in all areas, and to earn in power what their father had achieved in wealth, in order to fulfill their patriotic and philanthropic duty. Driven by ambition tempered with compassion, Joe and Rose Kennedy's two middle sons exceeded their parents' expectations, to become two of the most loved and respected figures in modern American history.

Opposite:
Jean, Pat, Bobby, Jack, and Eunice are all smiles in this undated photograph.

Above:
The Kennedy clan hams it up for the camera, Palm Beach, 1948. Pictured from left are Ted, Jean, Pat, Jack, Bobby (kneeling), and an unidentified friend (on the ground).

Joe and Rose Kennedy return to New York from a trip in 1928. By the late 1920s this grandson of poor Irish immigrants had made himself an extremely wealthy man.

Joe Jr., the oldest of the nine Kennedy children, with Jack, Rosemary, Kathleen, and Eunice, in 1925.

Left:

By 1934, the Kennedy clan was complete. Pictured left to right are (top row) John, Jean, and Robert, and (front row) Patricia, Rose, Joe Sr. holding Teddy, Kathleen, Eunice, and Rosemary. (Joe Jr. does not appear in this photo).

Above:

Wealthy and politically connected, the Kennedys had become one of the most distinguished families in the United States by 1941. Pictured are (left side, clockwise from left) Joe Sr., Patricia, Jack, Eunice, and Jean; and (right side, clockwise from left) Bobby, Kathleen, Rosemary, Joe Jr., Rose, and Ted.

Above, left:
A ten-year-old Jack in uniform for the Dexter School football team in Brookline, Massachusetts.

Above, right:
Bobby Kennedy in his Sunday best, Palm Beach, around 1934.

Opposite:
Jack with younger brothers, Teddy and Bobby, in Palm Beach, 1936.

Far left:

In 1939, during Joe Sr.'s tenure as U.S. ambassador to Great Britain, the entire Kennedy family traveled to the Vatican for a private audience with Pope Pius XII. Jack and Bobby appear at Rose's right.

Left:

In March of 1939, Jack accompanied his father to Rome, where Joe Sr., then U.S. ambassador to Great Britain, represented President Roosevelt at the coronation of Pope Pius XII.

Left:
Jack and his buddy Lem Billings harass little brother Bobby at the Palm Beach estate.

Opposite, top left:
A postcard from Joe Jr., traveling in Switzerland, to Jack at Harvard, 1939.

Opposite, top right:
Jack and Bobby in London, 1939. Eight years apart in age, Jack and Bobby were not very close as youngsters. After Joe Jr.'s death in World War II, the two grew closer, developing a strong adult relationship.

Opposite, bottom:
Joe Jr., Joe Sr., and Jack in Europe in 1938. Joe Sr.'s political aspirations rested squarely on the shoulders of his eldest son and namesake, who excelled both academically and athletically. Jack spent much of his early years in Joe's shadow.

Dear Brother,
    Switz
was marvelous.
Lest you forget
what your dear
Brother looks like
here I am ready
to do The Cresta
Run. 75 miles per
hour 6 inches off the ground

Mr. Jack Kennedy
United State
Cambridge
Massachusetts
U.S.A.

Above:
Jack with Rose and Eunice in Rio de Janeiro, 1941.

Right:
Jack in Venice, 1937. While Joe Sr. was serving as U.S. ambassador to Great Britain, Jack traveled throughout Europe, to learn about world affairs and gather information on his father's behalf.

Above:

Jack, standing far right, with the crew of PT 109, in July 1943. Jack was rejected by the U.S. Army in 1941 due to his weak back. He trained over the summer, gaining enough strength to be accepted by the U.S. Navy. During the war, Jack was instrumental in saving his crew when their boat was rammed by a Japanese destroyer.

Opposite, left:

After leading the crew of his destroyed torpedo boat to safety on a nearby island, Jack risked his life repeatedly over several days, swimming the surrounding waters in search of a rescue ship. He is pictured here examining the coconut on which he carved a message for help, which was carried off by helpful islanders.

Opposite, right:

Jack was awarded the Purple Heart and the Navy and Marine Corps Medal for his heroics in the Pacific. When asked years later how he became a hero, Jack replied, "It was involuntary. They sank my boat."

Above, left:
A portion of a 1945 letter from Bobby to Jack.

Above, right:
In 1946, Joe Sr. visited Bobby on board the USS *Joseph P. Kennedy, Jr.*

Opposite:
Seventeen-year-old Bobby is sworn in as a naval aviation cadet. Bobby left Harvard in 1944 to enlist. Poignantly, he would find himself assigned to the destroyer USS *Joseph P. Kennedy, Jr.,* named in honor of his brother, who was killed in a bombing mission that same year.

Above:
Jack, Jean, Rose, Joe Sr., Ted, Patricia, Bobby, and Eunice pose for the cameras during a family football game in Hyannis Port in autumn of 1948. Earlier that year, Kathleen was killed in a plane crash. Once again, the family held itself together through tragedy.

Opposite:
Tragedy hit the Kennedy family in 1944, when Joe Jr. (shown here with his plane), serving as a navy flyer in Europe, was killed in a midair explosion. Despite their grief and pain, the family continued looking forward, and Joe Sr.'s dreams and political ambitions were transferred to Jack.

PART TWO
LAYING FOUNDATIONS

Jack and Bobby both arrived on the Washington political scene quite young—Jack as a congressman in 1946 and Bobby as an attorney for the Justice Department in 1951. Jack developed a respectable non-partisan voting record, fighting for slum clearance and low-cost housing, while Bobby earned a reputation as an activist, prosecuting graft, income tax evasion, labor racketeering, and union corruption. Bobby took a leave of absence from the Justice department in 1952 to manage Jack's senatorial campaigns.

During the years preceding the presidential race of 1960, the two brothers were starting their own families, extending the Kennedy clan with in-laws and grandchildren. Bobby married his college sweetheart, Ethel Skakel, in 1950, and settled happily down into his life as a respectful husband and devoted father. Jack held on to bachelorhood a while longer, until he was swept away by the style and grace of Jacqueline Bouvier, whom he married in 1953. Poised to take center stage in Washington, D.C., in 1960, the two dynamic, attractive couples seemed to stand for a new golden age—which the press lost no time in dubbing Camelot.

Opposite:
With Jack and Bobby on the political fast track, and Teddy poised to continue the tradition, Joseph Kennedy's three boys had all the makings of an American dynasty in 1957.

Above:
Bobby took leave from his position as chief counsel for the Senate Investigations Committee to run Jack's congressional campaigns in the 1950s.

Left:
Bobby met Ethel Skakel in 1946, during his junior year at Harvard. They were married four years later.

Above:
Big brother and best man Jack examines the wedding cake, while Bobby and Ethel prepare for the ceremonial cutting. Like all the wives and husbands related by marriage to the Kennedy clan, Ethel became a "naturalized Kennedy," and an essential part of this close-knit family even years after Bobby's death.

Opposite:
Ethel and Bobby pose at their June 1950 wedding with bridesmaid Jean Kennedy.

Opposite:
Jack met Jacqueline Bouvier in 1952. He was a young senator, she was an inquiring photographer from the *Washington Times–Herald* sent to interview him.

Above:
Jack and Jackie were often referred to as the reigning king and queen of Camelot, the romantic, idealistic world of gallant knights and enchanting ladies. Both husband and wife were attractive and charming, and their youthful energy only added to their appeal.

In September of 1953, Jack's status as America's most eligible bachelor came to an end. Jacqueline Bouvier, rich in everything but money, fascinated Jack with her grace and style. Engaged through a telegram, they were married at St. Mary's Catholic Church in Newport, Rhode Island.

Left:
Jackie sees Jack off to work at the Senate, 1957. During the first few years of their marriage, Jackie nursed Jack through several serious illnesses. His injured back required major surgery once in 1954 and again in 1955.

Above and opposite:
Bonded by work, play, and family, Jack and Jackie and Bobby and Ethel seemed inseparable. They socialized together, as above, in Jack and Jackie's Georgetown home, and vacationed together as well in Palm Beach, opposite.

Opposite:
Taking in a day of sailing with Jackie, Ethel, and the children, Jack and Bobby enjoy some vacation time in Hyannis Port, 1959.

Left:
Jack and Bobby at Bobby and Ethel's Hickory Hill home. Following Joe Jr.'s death, Jack and Bobby became very close. As they matured and the gap in their ages became less significant, their relationship grew stronger, both as brothers and colleagues.

Above:
Jackie, Jack, Ethel, and Bobby pose with the Democratic Party mascot at Hickory Hill.

Above:

As committed as Bobby was to his career, he was first and foremost a family man. Here, he gives his five-year-old daughter, Kathleen, a spray with the hose, while her brothers Joseph and Bobby look on, June 1957.

Opposite:

Bobby loosens his tie and tends to his children, June 1957.

Opposite:
Jackie, Teddy, Jack, Ethel, Joe Sr., Bobby, Eunice, Steven Smith, and Jean pose for a portrait, Palm Beach, 1957.

Above:
As senator, Jack stood by his campaign promise to "do more for Massachusetts."

Opposite:
Jack and Bobby at Hickory Hill, 1957.

Above:
As their careers progressed, Jack and Bobby grew more reliant on each other's advice. During the Senate's 1957 investigations into labor racketeering, the two were virtually inseparable.

Above:
Jackie with daughter Caroline in Hyannis Port, 1959.

Right:
The brothers team up as tennis partners in Palm Beach, 1957.

Above:

Jack in a moment of reflection, Boston, 1957. Jack came close to gaining the nomination for vice president as Adlai Stevenson's running mate in 1956. By 1957, he was a clear front-runner for the Democratic presidential nomination for the next election.

Right:

Bobby sits alone in the Senate Caucus Room, after three weeks of hearings on labor union corruption in 1957.

Opposite:
Ted, Jack, and Bobby all decked out for the annual Grid Iron Club Dinner in Washington, D.C.

Above:
Bobby, Ted, and Jack confer during a committee hearing in 1959.

Right:
The brothers in front of the Capitol, 1957. By 1957 Jack was a clear contender for the presidential nomination, and his brother's role as manager, friend, and confidant was equally obvious.

PART THREE
ON THE CAMPAIGN TRAIL

In April of 1959, Bobby Kennedy sat at the head of his father's table in Palm Beach and set in motion the campaign to elect his brother Jack as the thirty-fifth president of the United States. Groomed for a life in politics, Jack Kennedy had spent the years since the 1956 elections traveling the country, attending functions, and making political friends.

Jack and Bobby proved to be an ideal pairing. Jack had political experience, an admirable military background, and a worthy congressional record. His natural charisma, humor, and charm had the power to sway voters to his side. Bobby proved to be a tireless and effective campaign manager. His complete confidence in his brother's abilities made Bobby utterly devoted to the task.

Opposite:
When the Kennedys campaigned, it was quite clear that politics was a family business. Here, Jack is joined by Bobby; Ethel; their children, Kathleen, Bobby, Joe, and David; and Jack and Bobby's nephew, Bobby Shriver, 1960.

Above:
Jack and Bobby go over last-minute strategy in a Los Angeles hotel room on the eve of the convention.

They formed an inseparable and effective political team. Despite their efforts and positive outlook for the future, the election turned out painfully close. Kennedy defeated Nixon by just under 115,000 votes. But by the time Jack Kennedy took the oath of office on January 20, 1961, the entire nation seemed ready to embrace him.

Above:
Jack and Bobby in an early morning huddle with Connecticut Governor John Baily (left) and state Democratic Chairman Bob Baily at the Democratic National Convention in Los Angeles, July 1960.

Opposite:
New York City's Columbus Day Parade was one of many stops along the campaign trail. Here, the crowd focuses on Jack and Jackie as the procession files past them up Fifth Avenue in October 1960.

Above, left:
The 1960 campaign effort shared by the two brothers in many ways foreshadowed the style of Jack's presidency. With Jack suffering from a sinus infection, Bobby addresses workers at the Brooklyn Navy Yard while Jack passes him notes.

Above, right:
Bobby was a natural political strategist, and ruled his brother's campaign with an iron will and ceaseless energy. Here, he attends to returns at his home on election night, 1960.

Opposite:
Jack campaigned extensively. Here, he addresses a crowd in Pennsylvania's Steel Valley.

Kennedy had not only financial connections, but also social ones, which helped to make him a household name. Here, he dines with Frank Sinatra at a fund-raising dinner the night before the Democratic National Convention, July 1960.

Left:
Bobby chats with his brother-in-law, actor Peter Lawford, and committee member Paul Ziffren at the 1960 convention.

Jack, Jackie, and daughter Caroline enjoy a
brief holiday at the Hyannis Port estate
during the 1960 campaign.

Above:

The family poses with the president-elect at Hyannis Port in November 1960. Seated, left to right, are Eunice, Rose, Joe, Jackie, and Ted. Standing, left to right, are Ethel; Jean's husband, Stephen Smith; Jean; Jack; Bobby; Patricia; Eunice's husband, Sargent Shriver; Ted's wife, Joan; and Patricia's husband, Peter Lawford.

Opposite:

Jack made history as the first president to nominate his brother to a high-ranking cabinet position. Outside his Georgetown home, in December 1960, Jack announces Bobby's appointment to the position of attorney general.

Right:

Frank Sinatra accompanies Jackie to a pre-Inauguration gala, January 1960.

Opposite:

Outgoing vice president and defeated presidential candidate Richard Nixon congratulates the newly inaugurated John F. Kennedy, while Vice President Lyndon B. Johnson looks on. Kennedy dedicated his inaugural address to foreign affairs and to the problem of poverty, and offered the unforgettable challenge to Americans: "... ask not what your country can do for you; ask what you can do for your country."

PART FOUR
ONE THOUSAND DAYS

When John F. Kennedy became the thirty-fifth President of the United States, he made history on many fronts. He was the first Roman Catholic president, and, at forty-three years of age, he was the youngest president ever elected. (Theodore Roosevelt was a few months younger when he replaced the deceased William McKinley in 1901.) As Jack's attorney general and most trusted advisor, Bobby, too, began to make his mark on the new administration. But only time would reveal the mettle of America's two determined, but as yet untested, young leaders. While Jack selected his cabinet, events were brewing in other parts of the world that would have an enormous impact on his administration. The Cuban missile crisis, which involved a stand-off between the Soviet Union and the United States so near our American shores, presented Jack Kennedy with one of his earliest and most monumental challenges.

Despite having been elected by one of the narrowest margins ever in a presidential race, the young, spirited president and his family enjoyed increasingly widespread public respect and support. The people became enamored of Jacqueline Kennedy, whose beauty, warmth, and intelligence set an absolute standard of elegance throughout the Western world. She and Jack became the king and queen of a modern-day Camelot, and Bobby a trusted knight in their court.

Opposite:
Civil rights took a great leap forward under the Kennedy presidency. Here, Jack and Bobby discuss racial tensions in Mississippi, October 1962.

Above:
The presidential portrait. Jack, a Roman Catholic, may have lost many votes in the 1960 election because of his religion. However, he quickly became one of the most popular leaders in American history.

Opposite:
In France, Jackie charmed the nation with her elegance, poise, and perfect command of the language. The French people were so enamored with the first lady that Jack jokingly introduced himself to the press as "the man who accompanied Mrs. Kennedy to France."

Above:
Seven-year-old Robert Kennedy, Jr., plays with a salamander he brought to the president during a visit to the White House in March 1961. Bobby Kennedy, Sr.'s presence in the White House was such a regular occurrence that photographers didn't even bother to photograph him there.

71

Opposite, top left:
Bobby had a unique ability to relate to the less fortunate despite his own affluent background. As chairman of the President's Committee on Delinquency, Bobby visits a New York City community center, August 1963.

Opposite, top right:
As Jack's unswervingly loyal brother, Bobby was more than just attorney general, he was Jack's closest advisor. With no hidden agenda on either side, the brothers worked intuitively as a unit. The President once said, "With Bobby I don't have to think about organization, I just show up."

Opposite, bottom:
Kennedy was committed to maintaining a free Berlin, which had been split between the Western Allies and the Soviets since negotiations broke down in 1948. In June 1963—less than two years after the Berlin wall went up—Kennedy addressed a cheering crowd in West Berlin, stating, "All free men, wherever they may live, are citizens of Berlin. And therefore, as a free man, I take pride in the words 'Ich bin ein Berliner.'"

Above:
Bobby, Jack, and Joe Sr. meet briefly at a Rhode Island airfield in October 1961. Jack was heading for Newport, while his father and brother were catching a flight to the family homestead at Hyannis Port.

Above:

The extended First Family at the christening of Bobby's son Christopher George, July 1963.

Right:

Jack's family captivated the media and the public alike. Here, Jackie smiles for the camera while holding John Jr., at a celebration for astronaut Gordon Cooper, May 1963.

Opposite:

John-John peeks out from beneath the president's desk while playing in the Oval Office. Some criticized Jack for using his children as photo opportunities in order to increase his popularity, but most people believed his willingness to have them photographed was a simple case of fatherly pride.

Opposite:

Bobby speaks to reporters while working late, May 1961, after martial law had been declared in Alabama in response to civil rights demonstrations. Bobby would prove to be a prominent advocate for African Americans. He persuaded Jack to support black leaders and condemn segregation.

Above:

In foreign affairs Jack straddled the road between the hawks and the doves more effectively than any politician before or since. While he took a firm military stand against the threat of communism, he also founded the Peace Corps in 1961, to aid the citizens of developing countries. The organization sent young volunteers for up to two years at a time to a host of Third World nations. Here, Jack talks to volunteers with his brother-in-law Sargent Shriver, co-founder of the Peace Corps.

Above, left:
The brothers confer on the the White House lawn. As Jack's closest advisor, Bobby was a regular presence at the White House.

Above, right:
Bobby was dedicated to his work, and was often caught with his sleeves rolled up, immersed in the job at hand. Here, he peeks his head out of his office to order coffee, while meeting with his aides to discuss strategies for enrolling two black students at the University of Alabama, June 1963.

Opposite:
The Kennedy brothers pose for a photo at the White House, 1963.

Above:

When Soviet missile bases were discovered under construction in Cuba in October 1962, Jack took a firm stance. He signed a naval and air quarantine on all offensive weapons headed for Cuba and readied the United States' armed forces for combat. The nation held its breath for a week, until the Soviets turned their Cuba-bound arms shipments around. Here, Jack signs the proclamation putting the arms embargo into effect.

Opposite:

Jack speaks to reporters, 1963. He had taken a moderate stance on civil rights early in his career, but had always expressed a moral commitment to the principle of racial equality. As president, faced with increasing public tensions arising from segregation, especially in the South, he was obliged to put his politics behind his beliefs.

Bobby holds up his son for photographers as the clan enjoys their free time at Hyannis Port in this rare 1963 photograph.

PART FIVE
TRAGEDY IN DALLAS

O n November 22, 1963, President John F. Kennedy's motorcade followed a parade route through Dallas, Texas. At 12:30 P.M., as the motorcade made its way through Dealey Plaza, shots rang out. President Kennedy was fatally wounded.

On that day, the United States, struck from within, like Camelot, lost its innocence. For millions of people, Jack Kennedy had represented all that was best about America. He had heard the voices of the disenfranchised, stood up to foreign provocation, and inspired Americans to believe that as a people we could meet any challenge and overcome any difficulty. With the assassination of President Kennedy we suddenly found ourselves in a dangerous world. In one horrifying moment, our very sense of nationhood was shattered. Our best self—strong, confident, compassionate, and smiling—was gone. One of America's brightest lights had been extinguished.

Opposite:
Jackie, holding the hands of her children, leads the procession from the Capitol after Jack's funeral.

Above:
The assassination of John F. Kennedy and the national period of mourning that followed bound Americans in a shared grief. Here, a seasoned newspaper photographer breaks down in tears at Jack's funeral.

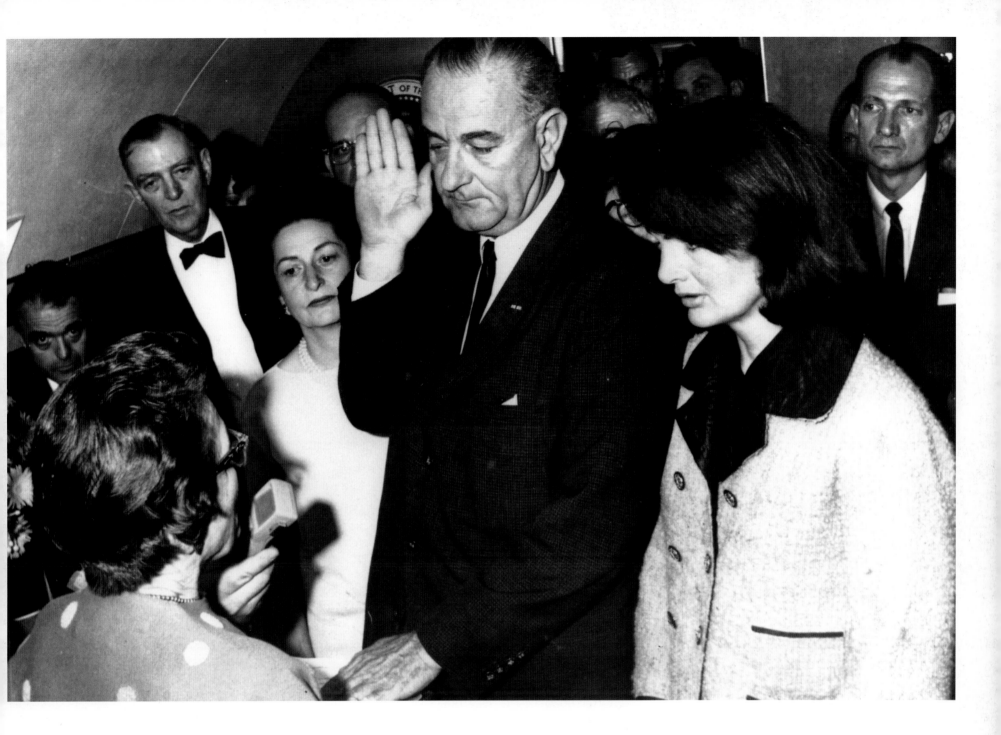

Opposite:
Jack and Jackie arrived in Dallas on the morning of November 22, 1963, and were welcomed by cheering, enthusiastic crowds. Here, the President's motorcade wends its way through Dealey Plaza just moments before the shots rang out.

Above:
Jack was pronounced dead within a half hour of his arrival at Parkland Memorial Hospital. A few hours later, a shocked Jackie stood by, still in her blood-stained suit, as Vice President Lyndon B. Johnson was sworn into office aboard Air Force One.

Right:

Jackie spent hours researching President Lincoln's funeral in planning the services for her husband. Here, Jack's casket is carried toward Arlington National Cemetery, followed by a riderless horse.

Opposite:

Bobby stood by Jackie throughout the ordeal of Jack's funeral. Although the entire world mourned, Jackie, Bobby, and the children would be alone with their loss.

The hearts of the nation broke as three-year-old John Kennedy, Jr., saluted his father's casket. Ted and Bobby remained by Jackie's side.

Above:
Four-year-old John F. Kennedy, Jr., shakes hands with Queen Elizabeth II at the ceremony for the dedication of Britain's memorial to Jack. Jackie, Caroline, and Bobby stand by.

Right:
Jackie stands in the doorway of her new Georgetown home, bidding farewell to Ethel and Bobby, who had helped her make the move from the White House after Jack's death. Jackie remained a vital part of the Kennedy family, even after she remarried five years later.

Opposite:
Jack's death had a profound effect on Bobby, who continued to pursue their shared vision for the nation as attorney general and, later, as senator. Here, Bobby visits his brother's grave in 1965, on what would have been Jack's forty-eighth birthday.

PART SIX
BOBBY ON HIS OWN

The intense shock of his brother's assassination drove Bobby Kennedy through misery and deep grief, to an equally profound shift in his world view. His beloved brother's death transformed him from a pragmatic liberal politician to a man moved by vision and conscience. More than ever before, he would address the causes of the suffering and injustices he saw corrupting the nation.

As attorney general, Bobby became a champion of the Bill of Rights. His humanity was stirred by Dr. Martin Luther King, Jr.'s struggle for civil rights. Bobby's tireless commitment to the American poor continued when he was elected to the Senate in 1964. He saw ghettos virtually side by side with million-dollar homes. He toured American schools where children arrived inadequately clothed and fed, and heard their lessons in substandard facilities. He reached out to the hopeless and the dispossessed throughout the country, and raised his own voice on their behalf. Bobby challenged the wealthy and powerful to see beyond their own doorstep, to feel beyond their own comfort, and to embrace fully the ideal that all men and women were created equal with certain inalienable rights under God.

Opposite:
Bobby walks alone toward the Capitol. As senator, Bobby continued to push for social change, and his bold commitment to doing the right thing won the hearts of many Americans.

Above:
Ted and Bobby with their father at Boston's Fenway Park during the opening game of the 1967 World Series.

Opposite:
Bobby paces in a fog-shrouded hospital parking lot, waiting for news, after his younger brother, Ted, was injured in a plane crash in 1964.

Above, left:
After Jack's death, Bobby stayed on as attorney general under Johnson despite his grief and his strained relationship with Johnson. Bobby took on the responsibility of seeing that the new president continued to pursue the goals of Jack's administration.

Above, right:
Bobby continued to crusade for racial equality under Johnson. The tension between Johnson and Bobby is evident in this photograph, taken as President Johnson signed the Civil Rights Act of 1964 into law.

Above:

Bobby with Dr. Martin Luther King, Jr., and Lyndon B. Johnson. Bobby's passionate embrace of civil rights for African Americans and his achievements in that respect remain his greatest political legacy.

Opposite:

Bobby became black America's strongest white voice, taking political risks that few government leaders were willing to chance at the time. Here, he observes a NAACP demonstration with Myrlie Evers, wife of slain leader Medgar Evers, and her children.

Above:

Bobby relocated to New York in 1964, after Johnson indicated that he would not be his choice for a running mate in that year. Here, with Ethel and his children, Bobby announces his candidacy for the state's vacant Senate seat.

Left:

Bobby in his Senate office. The painting behind his desk depicts his eldest brother, the late Joseph Kennedy, Jr., during World War II.

Opposite:

Campaigning under the slogan "Let's Put Bob Kennedy to Work for New York," Bobby found avid support among New Yorkers. Here, he campaigns on the streets of Brooklyn with vice-presidential candidate Hubert Humphrey, 1964.

Above:

Bobby was always a committed family man. His affection for his children was yet another reason for the public's tremendous esteem and affection. Here, photographers capture him at a dinner with four of his ten children, cutting meat for his young son, seated on his lap.

Opposite:

Jack's death was a permanent source of pain for Bobby, and he carried the loss with him for the rest of his life. Here, in White Horse, British Columbia, in 1965, he smiles after climbing the Canadian mountain named in honor of his murdered brother.

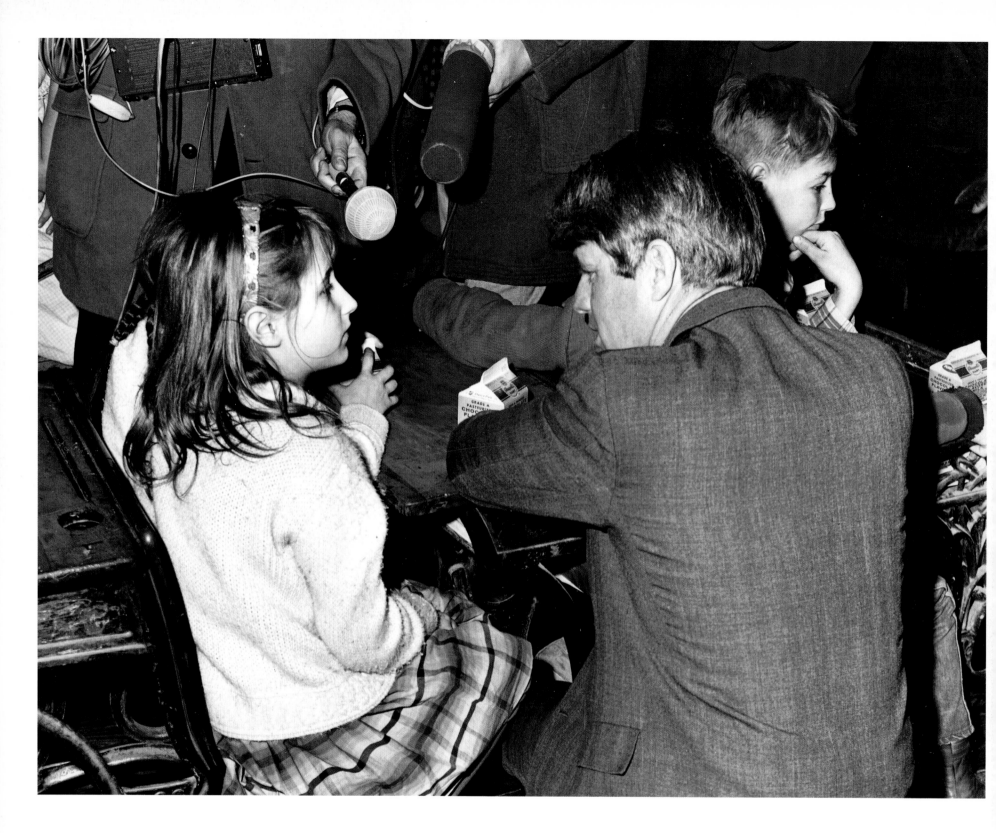

Above:

When Bobby toured the poverty-stricken regions of eastern Kentucky in 1968, he stopped by a one-room schoolhouse to talk with students. His ability to connect with the experience of impoverished Americans added to his appeal.

Opposite:

Though he lived what many would call a charmed life, free from financial worry, the many tragedies that he had lived through opened Bobby's eyes to the sufferings of others. When Bobby witnessed the conditions in which poor children lived, he was moved not only as a politician, but as a father.

PART SEVEN
A SECOND DREAM SHATTERED

Four years and a few months after Jack Kennedy was laid to rest, Bobby Kennedy decided to continue where his martyred brother had left off. News of his campaign for the presidency galvanized the nation. The political climate was turbulent, charged with hope for change.

Bobby's appeal as a presidential candidate was far different from the public image of his brother. Where Jack had been more of a stalwart, dependable hero, Bobby was seen as a man who would shake things up and fulfill the aspirations of a new and compassionate generation. After the years of disorientation and confusion following Jack's death, the country was experiencing a surge of vigor and excitement at the prospect of sending Bobby to the White House.

Opposite:
Before leaving the Ambassador Ballroom, Bobby thanked his supporters. A few minutes later, he was struck down by an assassin's bullet as he was leaving the building via the hotel's food service pantry.

Above:
Ethel leads the procession at Bobby's funeral in New York. Bobby left behind eleven children, the last of whom was born after he died.

On April 4, 1968, Bobby Kennedy was about to speak at a rally in a black ghetto in Indiana, when he received the appalling news of the assassination of Dr. Martin Luther King, Jr. His instinctive response was, "Oh, God, when is this violence going to stop?" He went on to address the crowd, whose deep sadness and rage he had experienced himself after the murder of his brother. He urged all Americans not to give in to the looming hatred, violence, and division, but to remember the teachings of Dr. King and John Kennedy and to work to fulfill their dreams for the nation.

Barely two months later, on June 5, 1968, Bobby Kennedy was gunned down after giving a victory speech in Los Angeles.

Bobby and Ethel greet crowds from the back of a train during the campaign. He was more generally popular than his brother had ever been, and seemed likely to win not only the Democratic presidential nomination, but the presidency itself.

Left and below:
Despite his brother's violent death, Bobby continued to make countless public appearances, often greeting crowds from open cars.

Opposite:
The presidential hopeful reaches out to a supporter, 1968. Some years earlier, Ben Bradlee of *Newsweek* had asked Jack why, beyond his family bond, he thought Bobby was so great. The president replied, "First, his high moral standards, strict personal ethics. He's a puritan, absolutely incorruptible. He's got compassion, a real sense of compassion."

INDEX

PHOTOGRAPHY CREDITS

The publishers have made every effort to trace the copyright owners of the illustrations in this book, but the nature of the material has meant that this has not always been possible. Any person or organization we have failed to reach, despite our efforts, is invited to contact the Photo Director.

AP / Wide World Photos: pp. 52, 53 left, 54, 56, 65, 118

©Burton Berinsky (Reproduced courtesy of Helene Berinsky): pp. 100 top, 102, 108–109, 112, 113

Corbis-Bettmann: p. 86

FPG International: pp. ©Photoworld: pp. 12, 34; ©Hy Peskin: p. 35; ©Pittsburgh Black Heritage: p. 59; ©T. Polumbaum: p. 62-63; ©AGIP-Robert Cohen: p. 70; ©Carl Moreus: p. 117 bottom

The John F. Kennedy Library: pp. 15 right; Kennedy Family Collection: pp. 16 right, 17; Presidential Collection: pp. 10, 11, 13, 21 top left, 21 bottom, 22–23 both, 24, 25 left, 27 right, 28, 29, 119; Courtesy of the RFK Museum: pp. 20, 27 left, 105; RFK Memorial: p. 32 both; Look Magazine Collection: pp. 6–7, 30, 31, 38 both, 39, 40, 41 both, 44, 45, 46, 47 all, 48–49 both, 50 left, 53 right, 74 right, 75, 77, 85; Cecil Stoughton: pp. 79, 82-83; A. Rowe: p. 98

©NYT Pictures: pp. 78 left, 100 bottom, 110 top; ©George Tames: p. 97 left

UPI / Corbis-Bettmann: pp. 2, 9, 14-15 left, 16 left, 18-19 both, 21 top right, 25 right, 26, 33, 36-37, 42, 43, 50 right-51, 55, 57, 58 both, 60, 61, 64, 66, 67, 68, 69, 71, 72 all, 73, 74 left, 76, 78 right, 80, 81, 84, 87, 88, 89, 90-91, 92 left, 93, 94, 95, 96, 97 right, 99, 101, 103, 104, 106, 107, 110 bottom, 111, 114, 115 both, 116 both, 117 top

Walz: UWE / Corbis: p. 92 right

AFTERWORD

Robert F. Kennedy's death marked the end of an era infused with optimism and confidence over which both he and Jack had presided. Jack and Bobby Kennedy will always be remembered for the significant achievements they made in the political and social realm. They brought us through the darkest days of the Cold War, and, among many of their forward-thinking ideas, left us with a still-vibrant Peace Corps, crucial civil rights legislation, and a remarkably successful space program.

But Jack and Bobby Kennedy also gave us something less tangible, though infinitely more important—a sense of possibility and hope for the future. Their legacies will stand the test of time. They will remain two uncommon heroes, larger than life, who gave us the courage to hold onto our ideals in the face of adversity and despair. As a people, we must be grateful for their sacrifices made on our behalf, for it is we who have been left to warm ourselves in the reflection of their splendor.

Opposite:
Washington, D.C., 1960.

Above:
Hyannis Port, 1948.

Opposite, left:
Well before Bobby's funeral on Friday morning, crowds began to form around New York City's St. Patrick's Cathedral and alongside the funeral procession route. Friends watched by the casket throughout the night. Coming so soon after the murder of Dr. Martin Luther King, Jr., Bobby's death left the nation numb. Yet another of the country's greatest, most inspiring leaders had met death at an assassin's hand.

Opposite, right:
Teddy delivers the eulogy for Bobby at St. Patrick's Cathedral.

Above:
As a young senator, John F. Kennedy once said, "Just as I went into politics because Joe died, if anything happened to me tomorrow, my brother Bobby would run for my seat in the Senate. And if Bobby died, Teddy would take over for him." Here, Teddy, the last of Joseph Kennedy's sons, accepts the flag that was draped over his brother Bobby's casket at Arlington National Cemetery.

Right:
Bobby's grave site at Arlington National Cemetery reflects his life—simple, pious, and clear.

Opposite:
Bobby gives the victory sign to a packed crowd of supporters at the Ambassador Hotel, after winning the California primary just after midnight, June 5, 1968. Having won five of the six primaries he entered, the road to the White House seemed like a smooth one.

Right, top:
A shocked Ethel Kennedy waits in the ambulance that carried her husband. The idea that the same fate that took Jack could take Bobby seemed impossible, but Ethel, her family, and the entire nation found themselves holding their breath once more.

Right, bottom:
Young people wait outside Good Samaritan Hospital on the morning of June 5th, awaiting news of Bobby's condition. Bobby died at 1:44 A.M. the next day.

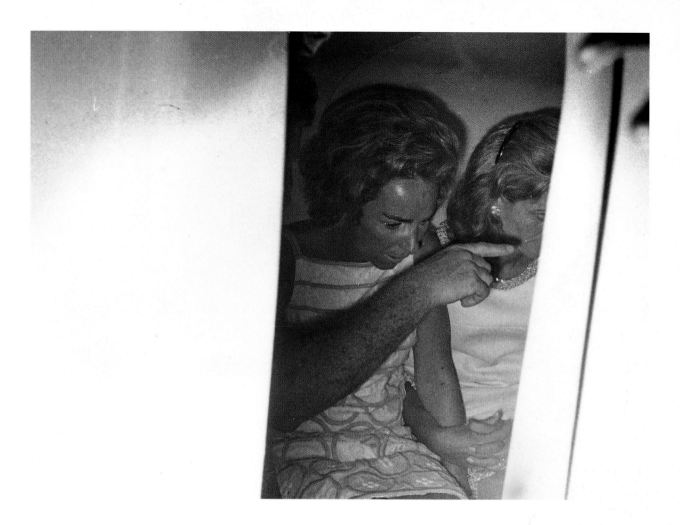

LOS ANGELES
Ambassador Hotel

Kenn

Bobby on the road during the 1968 campaign. As always, he kept up a demanding schedule and campaigned with boundless energy.

As Jack's campaign manager, Bobby gave everything he had. When he himself became the candidate, he worked even harder. Here he catches his breath for a moment between appearances on the road.